Staying Safe

Safety around Water

By MaryLee Knowlton
Photography by Gregg Andersen

Crabtree Publishing Company

www.crabtreebooks.com

Crabtree Publishing Company

www.crabtreebooks.com

Author: MaryLee Knowlton
Project coordinator: Robert Walker
Editor: Reagan Miller
Proofreaders: Molly Aloian, Crystal Sikkens
Production coordinator: Katherine Kantor
Prepress technicians: Samara Parent, Ken Wright
Design: Westgraphix/Tammy West

Written, developed, and produced by
Water Buffalo Books/Mark Sachner Publishing Services

Photographs: © Gregg Andersen/Gallery 19

Acknowledgments:
The publisher, producer, and photographer gratefully
acknowledge the following people for their participation
in the making of this book:
In Soldotna, Alaska: Dallas Armstrong, Mary Armstrong,
Chris Kempf, Er Kempf, Jackie Kempf, Etta Mae Near,
Jerome Near, Janet O'Toole, Mike O'Toole, John Pothast. In
Mankato, Minnesota: Debbie Benke, Candee Deichman, Liz
Goertzen, Syndie Johnson, Brianna Ostoff. And a special
thanks is offered to the dozens of school children, staff, and
parents who gave generously and enthusiastically of their
time and talent in the making of this book.

Library and Archives Canada Cataloguing in Publication

Knowlton, MaryLee, 1946-
    Safety around water / MaryLee Knowlton ; photography by Gregg Andersen.

(Staying safe)
Includes index.
ISBN 978-0-7787-4315-6 (bound).--ISBN 978-0-7787-4320-0 (pbk.).

    1. Swimming--Safety measures--Juvenile literature. 2. Safety
education--Juvenile literature. I. Andersen, Gregg II. Title.
III. Series: Staying safe (St. Catharines, Ont.)

GV838.53.S24K56 2008   j797.2'10289   C2008-905001-0

Library of Congress Cataloging-in-Publication Data

Knowlton, MaryLee, 1946-
    Safety around water / by MaryLee Knowlton ; photography by Gregg Andersen.
        p. cm. -- (Staying safe)
    Includes index.
    ISBN-13: 978-0-7787-4320-0 (pbk. : alk. paper)
    ISBN-10: 0-7787-4320-9 (pbk. : alk. paper)
    ISBN-13: 978-0-7787-4315-6 (reinforced library binding : alk. paper)
    ISBN-10: 0-7787-4315-2 (reinforced library binding : alk. paper)
    1. Swimming--Safety measures--Juvenile literature. 2. Swimming for children--Safety measures-
-Juvenile literature. 3. Aquatic sports--Safety measures--Juvenile literature. I. Andersen, Gregg,
ill. II. Title. III. Series.

    GV838.53.S24K67 2009
    797.2'1083--dc22
                                                    2008034151

Crabtree Publishing Company

www.crabtreebooks.com   1-800-387-7650

Published in Canada
Crabtree Publishing
616 Welland Ave.
St. Catharines, ON
L2M 5V6

Published in the United States
Crabtree Publishing
PMB16A
350 Fifth Ave., Suite 3308
New York, NY 10118

Published in the United Kingdom
Crabtree Publishing
White Cross Mills
High Town, Lancaster
LA1 4XS

Published in Australia
Crabtree Publishing
386 Mt. Alexander Rd.
Ascot Vale (Melbourne)
VIC 3032

Contents

Words in **bold** are defined in the glossary on page 30.

Staying Safe around Water

Every day, you have to make choices about your own safety. Whether you are at home, at school, at a playground, or around water, staying safe is something you must always think about.

In this book, each section presents a special water safety **hazard** or problem.

Here is how the book works:

First, you will read about a water safety problem.

Second, you will choose how to solve the problem.

Third, you will learn about the **consequence**, or outcome, of each choice.

For every bad consequence, you will see a "no" sign.

For every good consequence, you will see a gold star.

Finally, you will learn which is the best choice and why.

You will also learn important lessons about staying safe around water and being sure that others stay safe, too. Staying safe around water is a serious responsibility. But it can also mean having a lot of fun in the water!

Swimming Alone

Don't you love to go swimming? You can swim in a lake, in a swimming pool, or in an ocean. The water makes you feel cool and happy. Swimming and playing in the water is a great way to make friends and have fun.

Do you know the best way to have fun in the water and stay safe?

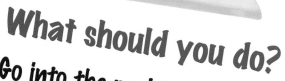

What's happening?

You can't wait to get into the water, but there are no grownups around.

What should you do?

A. Go into the pool but stay in the shallow end.

B. Ask an older kid to be your buddy and watch you.

C. Wait until a lifeguard, one of your parents, or another adult in charge of you comes to watch you swim.

Which is the best choice?

Turn the page ....➤ and find out!

What happens next:

If you choose A . . .

The water might be deeper than you think.
You could have trouble swimming.
You could even drown! 🚫

If you choose B . . .

Other kids are
not in charge of keeping you safe.
They won't know what to do in an emergency. 🚫

Adults in charge
of you will keep their eyes on
you all the time. You will stay safe!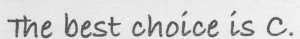

The best choice is C.
Wait until an adult in charge of you comes to
watch you swim.

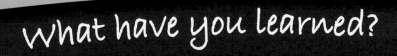

What have you learned?

You have learned the first rule of staying safe
when you are swimming: Always be sure that
a grownup in charge is watching you.

Running Around the Pool

Wet feet! Wet floors! People sitting around in chairs! Other kids all over the place! The area around a pool, indoors or outdoors, can be a very busy place.

How do you keep yourself and others safe on such a slippery **surface**?

What's happening?

You and your brother are playing in the pool. You see some friends at the other end of the pool. You can't wait to get over there to play with them.

What should you do?

A. Get your brother to jump out of the water and run with you to the other end of the pool to play.

B. Run to the other end of the pool by yourself to play with your friends.

C. Walk carefully or swim to the end of the pool to join your friends.

Which is the best choice?

Turn the page ....➤ and find out!

What happens next:

If you choose A . . .

While running, your brother might fall and you could trip over him! 🚫

If you choose B . . .

You might slip and fall and scrape your leg. You may have to stop swimming! 🚫

If you choose C . . .

You join your friends, you know how deep the water is, and you stay safe!

The best choice is C.
Walk carefully or swim to the end of the pool with your brother to join your friends. You should also tell an adult in charge that you are going to the other side of the pool.

What have you learned?

The floors around the pool are always slippery and hard. Never run around the pool. You can fall and hurt yourself or others. You could also fall or knock someone else into the pool. Always walk carefully in the pool area.

Jumping Too Close

Swimming in a pool that allows jumping is great fun. Flying through the air to land with a splash is one of the joys of swimming.

How can you jump safely so you do not hurt yourself or other swimmers?

What's happening?

You want to show your sister what a huge splash you can make when you do a cannonball.

What should you do?

A. Jump as close to her as you can get so she really notices that splash.

B. Yell to her to watch you as you jump toward another part of the pool.

C. Pick a spot where no one is swimming and where you have been before so you know how deep it is.

Which is the best choice?

Turn the page ....→
and find out!

What happens next:

If you choose A . . .

You might land on your sister and both of you could get hurt! 🚫

If you choose B . . .

You haven't looked before leaping, and you might scare other kids and get kicked out of the pool! 🚫

You haven't hurt anyone or ruined their fun, and your splash is awesome!

The best choice is C.
Pick a spot where no one is swimming and where you have been before so you know how deep it is.

What have you learned?

Jumping on people in the pool is very dangerous. Be sure to watch where you are jumping. The swimming pool is not a good place to surprise someone by landing too close. Make your big splash safely away from others.

How Deep Is It?

You really want to jump into the lake, but you don't know how deep the water is. If it's too shallow, you may hit the bottom and hurt yourself. If it's too deep, however, you may be out too far over your head. You could have trouble swimming back in to where you can stand.

How can you tell how deep the water is?

What's happening?

You are visiting your cousins at their **cottage** on the lake, and you can't wait to dive off the end of the **dock**.

What should you do?

A. Take a running dive off the end of the dock.

B. Look into the water to see if it is deep before you dive.

C. Ask an adult in charge if it's safe to dive in from the dock and if he or she will watch you.

Which is the best choice?

Turn the page............
and find out!

What happens next:

If you choose A . . .

The water might be very shallow. You could get hurt if you crash into the bottom of the lake! 🚫

If you choose B . . .

The water might be very deep and you could wind up farther from the safe area near the shore than you expected. You could be too far out to get back! 🚫

The adult tells you if it is safe to dive from the dock and shows you where you can swim while he or she watches you.

The best choice is C.
Ask an adult in charge if it's safe to dive in from the dock and if he or she will watch you.

What have you learned?

Never dive into water until an adult tells you it is safe for swimming and agrees to stay and watch while you swim. What you can't see in the water can hurt you!

Pushing and Pulling

Staying safe in the water means being able to breathe and to move your arms and legs. Other swimmers need to decide when and where they will go in water. They need to trust you to let them breathe and move around so they feel safe and comfortable. The pool is a good place to show others that you know how to treat them with respect.

What's the best way to treat others so they can feel safe and trust you in the water?

What's happening?

You want to swim, splash, and play in the water with your cousin.

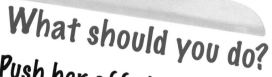

What should you do?

A. Push her off the edge into the water and then jump in after her.

B. Swim under her and pull her under by her legs.

C. Stand with her in the shallow end and ask her if she'd like to play.

Which is the best choice?

Turn the page·········➔
and find out!

What happens next:

If you choose A . . .

She might get scared. If the water is over her head and she's not wearing a life jacket, she might have trouble staying afloat. She might need to be rescued! 🚫

If you choose B . . .

She might have trouble breathing. She could get scared and breathe in water or kick you in the face. She might also tell a grownup. You could get kicked out of the pool! 🚫

You find out what she'd like
to do in the water. She may just want to
play safely in the shallow end of the pool.

The best choice is C.

Your cousin decides what she wants to do. She
can get a life jacket from a grownup in charge or
stay near the side at the shallow end of the pool.

What have you learned?

Never push anyone in or near the water. Never
pull or hold anybody so they cannot move the
way they need to. Surprises in the water are
never good surprises!

Playing Around Water

The way water moves in rivers and streams is called its **current**. When snow melts or rain falls, the current in a small stream may be faster and stronger than usual. The water may be deeper than usual, too. **Bluffs** and **banks** may be slippery or crumbly under your feet.

How do you know if it's safe to play around a river or stream?

What's happening?

You think the stream in the park would be a great place to sail the paper boats you and your sister made during the last three days when it rained.

What should you do?

A. Walk into the shallow part of the stream and release your boats.

B. Carefully creep down the bank of the stream, lean over the water's edge, and drop your boats into the stream.

C. Talk to a grownup who takes care of you and let him or her decide if it is okay to sail boats and how to do it safely while he or she watches.

Which is the best choice?

Turn the page and find out!

What happens next:

If you choose A . . .

The current in the stream might knock your feet out from under you and sweep you away in the water. 🚫

If you choose B . . .

The banks of the stream might crumble under your feet and you could fall into the water. 🚫

The grownup takes you to a pond or some other safe place away from moving or deep water where you can sail your boats.

The best choice is C.

Ask a grownup who takes care of you if it is safe to sail boats and find out how to do it safely while he or she watches you. You will stay safe, and your boats won't be swept away either!

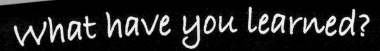

What have you learned?

Never go near a river, stream, pond, or lake without an adult to watch over you especially after a rainstorm, when they become deeper and faster than usual.

Glossary

bank The land that slopes down toward a river or stream

bluffs Steep cliffs or banks that drop off suddenly to the water below

buddy In swimming, a partner who stays with you so either of you can help the other one in case of an emergency

cannonball A dive in which you roll yourself up into a ball and make a huge splash

consequence The outcome or effect of an action; a thing that happens as a result of something else happening

current The part of a river or stream that moves swiftly in one direction

cottage A small house that people usually stay in for a vacation

dock A platform or pier sticking out into the water that is usually used as a landing place for boats

hazard A danger or a chance to get hurt

surface The outer or topmost layer of a liquid or solid object

BOOKS

Signs at the Pool (Welcome Books: Signs in My World)
Mary Hill. Children's Press, 2003.

Water Safety (Be Safe!). Peggy Pancella. Heinemann, 2005.

Watch Out! Near Water (Watch Out! Books). Claire Llewellyn.
Barron's Educational Series, 2006.

Water Safety (Stay Safe!). Sue Barraclough. Heinemann, 2007.

WEBSITES

Kids Health: For Kids: Swimming
http://kidshealth.org/kid/watch/out/water.html
Tons of tips for staying safe at the water park, the pool,
and the beach.

Safe Kids USA: Water Safety Campaign 2008
http://www.usa.safekids.org/water
Whether it's at the beach, on boats, in pools and hot tubs, or
at home, this kids' guide to being safe rallies around the slogan
"Kids Don't Float."

Splash Zone USA: Teaching Kids about Water Safety
http://www.splashzoneusa.com/home.html
Hosted by Sonny, the friendliest fish around, and Bubbles, your
safe hot tub buddy, this interactive site alerts kids to safe water
practices in pools and hot tubs with games, contests, and puzzles.

Index

B
Banks 26, 27, 28
Bluffs 26
Breathing 22, 23
Buddies and friends
7, 11, 13

C
Cannonballs 15
Current 26, 28

D
Deep water 8, 13,
15, 17, 18, 20,
26, 29
Docks 19, 21
Drowning 8

F
Falling 12, 13
First rule of staying
safe 9

G
Grownups and
adults 7, 9, 13,
19, 21, 24, 25,
27, 29

H
Holding 25

J
Jumping and diving
11, 14–17,
18–21, 23

L
Lakes 6, 18-21, 29
Lifeguards 7
Life jackets 24, 25

O
Ocean 6

P
Ponds 29
Pulling 22, 23, 25
Pushing 22, 23, 25

R
Rain 26, 27, 29
Respect 22
Rivers 26, 29
Running 10–13, 19

S
Shallow water 7, 18,
20, 23, 25, 27
Slippery surfaces
10, 12, 13, 26
Splashing 14, 15,
17, 23
Streams 26–29
Swimming 6, 7,
8, 9, 11, 12, 13,
14, 15, 17, 18, 21,
22, 23
Swimming pools
6, 7, 10, 11, 13,
14–17, 22–25

T
Trust 22

W
Walking 11, 13

Printed in the U.S.A.